D0716957

A BOOK OF INSIGHT

A Guide for the Advanced Soul

A BOOK OF INSIGHT

A Guide for the Advanced Soul

HOW TO USE THIS GUIDE

You have a problem or need guidance to help you make a decision. Picture this clearly in your mind; meditate on it so that the mind gradually subsides into stillness. This allows you to draw on your subconscious and intuitive powers to respond.

Now put forward your request while randomly opening the book. The first words you read will tell you what you most need to hear.

Clearly it is your interpretation of the quotation that will give you your answer. Be open to what you read: interpreting it objectively, and without projecting your wishes on the outcome. The value of the reading will depend on how far you are willing to change in the direction indicated. Opposing the forces controlling your life creates disharmony around you.

Knowing that you create your personal reality is most important, because this enables you to understand that all exterior circumstances, events and experiences in the world flow from the centre of your being to provide a living feedback.

What is written in this book will tell you everything you need to know. At this instant you are a reflection of the universe where all things and events exist simultaneously - the past, present, and the future juxtaposed - and you contain all the potentialities of the whole world within you. Your guidance is here for you to work with from the point of your own reality.

Other Inspirational Books
by Susan Hayward

BEGIN IT NOW
Motivational Quotations
ISBN 09590439 1 8

BAG OF JEWELS
Metaphysical Quotations
ISBN 09590439 5 0

Published by In-Tune Books.
Available through Ingram Book Distribution.

A BOOK OF INSIGHT

A Guide
for the
Advanced Soul

Created & Handwritten by

SUSAN HAYWARD

IN·TUNE BOOKS

IN-TUNE BOOKS
PO BOX 193
AVALON NSW 2107
AUSTRALIA
email mcohan@ozemail.com.au

First published in Hardcover February 1985.
Paperback edition May 1990.

Quotations Calligraphy by Susan Hayward.
Jacket design by Margo Snape.
Endpapers by Margo Snape.

Produced by Phoenix Offset, HK.

ISBN 09590439 3 4

By the same author:

Begin It Now   1987 09590439 4 2
Bag of Jewels   1987 09590439 5 0
BEING - Reminders from the Gods   1997 09590439 8 5

INTERNATIONAL DISTRIBUTORS:

AUST: HarperCollins, Sydney
NZ: HarperCollins, Auckland
UK: Tiptree Distribution (TBS) Essex
USA: Bookpeople, New Leaf, Ingrams,
SA: Alternate Books, Johannesburg
INTERNET: Amazon.com
MAIL ORDER Australia: Adyar Bookshop (02) 9267 8509

A Letter to You

Dear Friend:

I have created this book for you to consult when you are faced with problems. It is a collection of beautiful words of wisdom that will guide and inspire you.

See yourself as part of the never-ending cycle of change in the universe and this book will reflect that change for you. Everything in the universe is continuously integrating and disintegrating— this produces transformation and growth. Your problems are caused by your resistance towards this natural cyclic movement of life.

When you randomly open this Guide you are addressing the universe, and it responds to your question, which you then interpret intuitively. Regard your problems as opportunities for learning and creating something new, and you will feel a sense of well-being that results from your shift in consciousness. Know that we are only presented with lessons when we are ready to learn them.

Above all, trust your own direction. I hope this Guide gives you confidence to follow your path and surrender to the inner intuitive voice that recognises the harmony and wholeness that has always been there.

I hope also that this contributes to the increasing new awareness and social transformation taking place throughout the world, that will unite all human beings as One.

Love,
Susan

Life is the movie
   you see
      through your own,
         unique eyes.

It makes little difference
   what's happening out there,

      It's how you take it that counts.

DENIS WAITLEY
The Winner's Edge

Set your sights high,
   the higher the better.

Expect the most wonderful things
   to happen, not in the future
   but right now.

Realise that nothing is too good.

Allow absolutely nothing
   to hamper you
   or hold you up
      in any way.

EILEEN CADDY
Footprints on the Path

*To see your drama
clearly
is to be liberated
from it.*

KEN KEYES, JR
Handbook to Higher Consciousness

A human being
is a single being.

Unique
and unrepeatable.

JOHN PAUL II

Have no fear
    of moving into the unknown.
Simply step out fearlessly
    knowing that I am with you,
    therefore no harm can befall you;
        all is very very well.

Do this in complete faith
    and confidence.

EILEEN CADDY
Footprints on the Path

/·)

Life is a series
  of natural
   and spontaneous
      changes.

Don't resist them —
        that only creates sorrow.

Let reality be reality.

Let things flow naturally forward
  in whatever way
     they like.

LAO-TSE

Experience
is determined by yourself -

not the circumstances
of your life.

GITA BELLIN

When you feel
    that you have reached the end
and that you cannot go
            one step further,
when life seems to be
    drained of all purpose:

What a wonderful opportunity
    to start all over again,
        to turn over a new page.

EILEEN CADDY
Footprints on the Path

To find yourself,

Think for yourself.

SOCRATES

A tree that can fill the span
  of a man's arms
  grows from a downy tip;

A terrace nine storeys high
  rises from hodfuls of earth;

A journey of a thousand miles
  starts from beneath one's feet.

LAO-TZU

Stride forward
    with a firm, steady step
    knowing with
        a deep, certain
            inner knowing
    that you will reach
    every goal you set yourselves,
    that you will achieve
            every aim.

EILEEN CADDY
Footprints on the Path

When you affirm your own
rightness in the universe,
then you co-operate with others easily
and automatically
as part of your own nature.

You, being yourself,
help others
be themselves.

Because you recognise
your own uniqueness
you will not need
to dominate others,
nor cringe before them.

JANE ROBERTS
The Nature of Personal Reality

Inner peace
 can be reached
  only when we practice
   forgiveness.

Forgiveness
 is the letting go of the past,
  and is therefore
   the means for correcting
    our misperceptions.

GERALD G. JAMPOLSKY
Love is Letting Go of Fear

Never be afraid
   to tread the path alone.

Know which is your path
   and follow it wherever
   it may lead you;

do not feel you have to follow
   in someone else's
                footsteps.

EILEEN CADDY
Footprints on the Path

The impossible is possible
when people align with you.

When you do things with people,
not against them,
the amazing resources
of the Higher Self within
are mobilised.

GITA BELLIN

Be open to your
happiness
and sadness
as they arise.

JOHN & LYN ST·CLAIR THOMAS
Eyes of the Beholder

Live
and work
but do not forget to play,
to have fun in life
and really enjoy it.

EILEEN CADDY
The Dawn of Change

Love alone can unite living beings
so as to complete and fulfill them...
for it alone joins them
by what is deepest
in themselves.

All we need is to imagine
our ability to love developing
until it embraces
the totality of men
and of the earth.

TEILHARD DE CHARDIN

However many holy words
you read,
however many you speak,
What good will they do you
if you do not act upon them?

THE DHAMMAPADA

Dwell not on the past.
Use it to illustrate a point,
then leave it behind.
Nothing really matters
except what you do now
in this instant of time.

From this moment onward
you can be an entirely different person,
filled with love and understanding,
ready with an outstretched hand,
uplifted and positive
in every thought
and deed.

EILEEN CADDY
God Spoke to Me

Until one is committed, there is hesitancy, the chance to draw back, always ineffectiveness. Concerning all acts of initiative (and creation), there is one elementary truth, the ignorance of which kills countless ideas and splendid plans: that the moment one definitely commits oneself, then Providence moves too.

All sorts of things occur to help one that would never otherwise have occurred. A whole stream of events issues from the decision, raising in one's favour all manner of unforeseen incidents and meetings and material assistance, which no man could have dreamed would have come his way.

SCOTTISH HIMALAYAN
EXPEDITION

Whatever you can do
or dream you can,
begin it.

Boldness has genius, magic
and power in it.

Begin it now.

GOETHE

All we
see or
seem
is but a dream
within
a
dream.

EDGAR ALLEN POE

Yesterday
  is but today's memory
      and
Tomorrow
  is today's dream.

KAHLIL GIBRAN
The Prophet

We are what we think.
All that we are
arises with our thoughts.
With our thoughts we make
the world.

Speak or act with a pure mind
and happiness will follow you
as your shadow,
unshakeable.

THE DHAMMAPADA

*A soul without
a high aim
is like a ship
without a rudder.*

EILEEN CADDY
The Dawn of Change

It is good to have an end
to journey towards,
but it is the journey that matters,
in the end.

URSULA LE GUIN
The Left Hand of Darkness

Cease trying
    to work everything out
        with your minds,
            it will get you nowhere.

Live by intuition
    and inspiration
        and let your whole life
            be a Revelation.

EILEEN CADDY
Footprints on the Path

The fates lead
  him who will—

    him who won't,
      they drag.

SENECA

Confine yourself
to
the
present.

MARCUS AURELIUS

Seek always
for the answer within.

Be not influenced
by those around you,
by their thoughts
or their words.

EILEEN CADDY
God Spoke to Me

Man cannot discover new oceans
until he has courage
to lose sight
of the shore.

UNKNOWN

I do not expect anything
from others,
So their actions
cannot be in opposition
to wishes of mine.

SWAMI SRI YUKTESWAR
Autobiography of a Yogi

*Your questions
indicate the depth
of your belief.*

*Look at the depth
of your questions.*

JOHN & LYN ST. CLAIR THOMAS
Eyes of the Beholder

The secret of making
   something work in your lives is,
first of all,
      the deep desire to make it work:

then the faith and belief
      that it can work:

then to hold that clear definite
vision in your consciousness
and see it working out
      step by step,
         without one thought
            of doubt or disbelief.

EILEEN CADDY
Footprints on the Path

Life is full
and overflowing
with the new.

But it is necessary to empty out
the old to make room
for the new to enter.

EILEEN CADDY
Footprints on the Path

Only in relationship can you
know yourself, not in abstraction
and certainly not in isolation.

The movement of behaviour
is the sure guide to yourself, it's
the mirror of your consciousness;
this mirror will reveal its content,
the images, the attachments, the
fears, the loneliness, the joy and
sorrow.

Poverty lies in running away
from this, either in its
sublimations or its identities.

J. KRISHNAMURTI

You make
yourself and
others suffer
just as much
when

you take offense

as when
you give offense.

KEN KEYES, JR
Handbook to Higher Consciousness

The more you depend
on forces
outside yourself,
the more you are dominated
by them.

HAROLD SHERMAN

The most effective way
to achieve right relations
with any living thing
is to look for the best in it,
and then help that best
into the fullest expression.

J. ALLEN BOONE
Kinship with All Life

Let there be more
joy and laughter
in your living.

EILEEN CADDY
God Spoke to Me

Thoughts are things;
     they have tremendous power.

Thoughts of doubt and fear are pathways
     to failure.
When you conquer negative attitudes
    of doubt and fear you conquer failure.

Thoughts crystallize into habit
    and habit solidifies into circumstances.

BRIAN ADAMS
How To Succeed

You are given the gifts of the gods;
   you create your reality
   according to your beliefs.

Yours is the creative energy
   that makes your world.

There are no limitations
   to the self
   except those you believe in.

JANE ROBERTS
The Nature of Personal Reality

A thing is complete
when you can
let it
be.

GITA BELLIN

There is only one courage
and that is the courage
to go on dying to the past,
not to collect it,
not to accumulate it,
not to cling to it.

We all cling to the past,
and because we cling
to the past we become
unavailable
to the present.

BHAGWAN SHREE RAJNEESH
Walking in Zen, Sitting in Zen

The past
    is dead

The future
    is imaginary

Happiness
    can only be

in the Eternal

        Now

        Moment

KEN KEYES, JR
Handbook to Higher Consciousness

One cannot conquer the evil in
himself by resisting it...
but by transmuting its energies
into other forms.

The energy that expresses
itself in the form of evil
is the same energy
which expresses itself
in the form of good;
and thus the one may
be transmuted into the other.

CHARLES HENRY MACKINTOSH
I Looked on Life

Be afraid of nothing
you have within you—
all wisdom
all power
all strength
all understanding.

EILEEN CADDY
The Dawn of Change

*If you know
    you want it,
        Have it.*

GITA BELLIN

Expect your every need
to be met,
expect the answer
to every problem,
expect abundance
on every level,
expect to grow spiritually.

EILEEN CADDY
The Dawn of Change

Ask, and it shall be given you;
seek, and ye shall find;
knock, and it shall be opened
unto you.

For every one that asketh,
receiveth;
and he that seeketh,
findeth;
and to him that knocketh
it shall be opened.

MATTHEW 7:7,8

At any moment
I could start being a
better person–

but which moment
should I choose ?

ASHLEIGH BRILLIANT
Potshots No. 1521

One has just to be oneself.
That's my basic message.

The moment you accept yourself
as you are,
all burdens,
all mountainous burdens
simply disappear.

Then life is a sheer joy,
a festival of lights.

BHAGWAN SHREE RAJNEESH
The Sound of One Hand Clapping

When you are inspired by some great
purpose, some extraordinary project,
all your thoughts break their bonds;
Your mind transcends limitations,
your consciousness expands in every direction,
and you find yourself in a new, great
and wonderful world.
Dormant forces, faculties and talents
become alive, and you discover yourself
to be a greater person by far
than you ever dreamed
yourself to be.

PATANJALI

'For those who believe,
no proof is necessary.

'For those who don't believe,
no proof is possible.

JOHN & LYN ST. CLAIR THOMAS
'Eyes of the Beholder

Take the good until you find something better, and in search for something better do not let the good slip away from you or die out. If you disregard it despite its worth, and pursue something better, what you had escapes you; but if you remain attached to what is good, you will always have it if nothing better follows.

PARACELSUS

We learn wisdom from failure
much more than from success:
We often discover what will do,
by finding out what will not do:
and probably he who never made a mistake
never made a discovery.

SAMUEL SMILES

Like attracts like.

*Whatever the conscious mind
thinks and believes,
the subconscious
identically
creates.*

BRIAN ADAMS
How To Succeed

The course of human life is like that of a great river which, by the force of its own swiftness, takes quite new and unforeseen channels where before there was no current— such varied currents and unpremeditated changes are part of God's purpose for our lives.

Life is not an artificial canal to be confined within prescribed channels.

When once this is clearly seen in our own lives, then we shall not be able to be misled by any mere fabrications.

RABINDRANATH TAGORE

Be at peace
and see
a clear pattern and plan
running through
all your lives.

Nothing is by chance.

EILEEN CADDY
Footprints on the Path

When love beckons to you, follow him.
    Though his ways are hard and steep.
And when his wings enfold you,
                yield to him,
    Though the sword hidden
among his pinions may wound you.

    And when he speaks to you,
      believe in him.
Though his voice may shatter your dreams
      as the north wind
        lays waste the garden.

KAHLIL GIBRAN
The Prophet

Life is either
  a daring adventure
    or nothing.

HELEN KELLER

There is no situation that could
    ever confront you
        that cannot be solved.
            Life takes on real meaning
                when you set values
                    for yourself,
                        regard yourself as worthwhile
                        and elevate your thoughts
                        to things that are of God-good.
            There is a Higher Power.
        Turn to it and use it;
It is yours for the asking.

BRIAN ADAMS
How To Succeed

Trials are but lessons
that you failed to learn
presented once again,
so where you made a faulty choice before
you can now make a better one,
and thus escape all pain
that what you chose before
has brought to you.

A COURSE IN MIRACLES

To every thing
there is a season,
and a time to every purpose
under the heaven.

ECCLESIASTES 3:1

*Everything
  we do in life...*

Is it not just a game ?

GURURAJ ANANDA YOGI

Every now and then go away,
  have a little relaxation,
  for when you come back
  to your work
  your judgement will be surer;
  since to remain constantly at work
  will cause you to lose power
                of judgement ...

Go some distance away
  because the work appears smaller
  and more of it
  can be taken in at a glance,
  and a lack of harmony
  or proportion
                is more readily seen.

LEONARDO DA VINCI

Change
is never a loss –

it is change only.

VERNON HOWARD
The Mystic Path to Cosmic Power

If you would learn
the secret
of right relations
look only for the divine
in people and things,
and leave all the rest to God.

J. ALLEN BOONE
Kinship with all Life

We can only
Be Here Now
when we accept instantly
our moment-by-moment
emotional experience.

GITA BELLIN

The greater
    the emphasis
        upon perfection
the further it recedes.

HARIDAS CHAUDHURI
Mastering the Problems of Living

That which oppresses me,
   is it my soul
   trying to come
   out in the open,
or the soul of the world
knocking at my heart
for its entrance ?

RABINDRANATH TAGORE

Why destroy
   your present happiness
      by a distant misery,
         which may never
            come at all ?

For every substantial grief
   has twenty shadows
      and most of the shadows
         are of your own making.

SYDNEY SMITH

You find true joy
  and happiness in life
when you give
  and give
    and go on giving
      and never count the cost.

EILEEN CADDY
The Dawn of Change

Success is a journey
not a destination –
half the fun is getting there.

GITA BELLIN

My life is a performance
for which
I was never given
any chance to rehearse.

ASHLEIGH BRILLIANT
Potshots No. 1318

Just look next time you are having some trip and riding a problem - just watch. Just stand aside and look at the problem. Is it really there? Or have you created it?

Look deeply into it, and you will suddenly see it is not increasing, it is decreasing; it is becoming smaller and smaller.

The more you put your energy into observation, the smaller it becomes. And a moment comes when suddenly it is not there... you will have a good laugh.

BHAGWAN SHREE RAJNEESH
The Tantra Vision Vol. I

Great spirits
have always encountered
violent opposition
from mediocre minds.

ALBERT EINSTEIN

Forgiveness recognises
what you thought
your brother did to you
has not occurred.

A COURSE IN MIRACLES

Learn to be silent.

Let your
    quiet mind
        listen
            and absorb.

PYTHAGORUS

Every issue,
belief,
attitude
or assumption
is precisely the issue
that stands between
you and your relationship
to another human being;
and between you
and yourself.

GITA BELLIN

Perfect kindness
acts
without thinking
of kindness.

LAO-TSE

Time is an invention.
Now is a reality.
So much creativity is happening
for the simple reason that we
have withdrawn ourselves
from past and future.

Our whole energy remains blocked
either in the past or in the future.

When you withdraw all your energy
from past and future a
tremendous explosion happens.

That explosion is creativity.

BHAGWAN SHREE RAJNEESH
The Goose Is Out

Of a certainty
the man who can see
all creatures in himself,
himself in all creatures,
knows no sorrow.

EESHA UPANISHAD

Every moment of your life
is infinitely creative
and the universe
is endlessly bountiful.

Just put forth
a clear enough request,
and everything
your heart desires
must come to you.

SHAKTI GAWAIN
Creative Visualisation

'Expand
in consciousness –
be ready to accept anything
now,
at any time.

EILEEN CADDY
God Spoke to Me

What we are today
  comes from
  our thoughts of yesterday,
  and our present thoughts
  build our life
  of tomorrow:

Our life is the creation of our mind.

THE BUDDHA

Love is

letting go

of fear.

GERALD JAMPOLSKY

When some misfortune threatens, consider seriously and deliberately what is the very worst that could possibly happen. Having looked this possible misfortune in the face, give yourself sound reasons for thinking that after all it would be no such terrible disaster. Such reasons always exist, since at the worst nothing that happens to oneself has any cosmic importance. When you have looked for some time steadily at the worst possibility and have said to yourself with real conviction, 'Well, after all, that would not matter so very much,' you will find that your worry diminishes to a quite extraordinary extent. It may be necessary to repeat the process a few times, but in the end, if you have shirked nothing in facing the worst possible issue, you will find that your worry disappears altogether and is replaced by a kind of exhilaration.

BERTRAND RUSSELL
The Conquest of Happiness

How much longer will you go on
  letting your energy sleep?

How much longer are you going
  to stay oblivious of the immensity
  of yourself?

Don't lose time in conflict;
  lose no time in doubt –
  time can never be recovered
  and if you miss an opportunity
  it may take many lives
  before another comes
  your way again.

BHAGWAN SHREE RAJNEESH
A Cup Of Tea

If you attack apparent negativity
            with negativity,
     you merely feed
  and inflame the source.

It's always best
  to take the positive
  in any conflict.

            If you genuinely love,
        or at least
      send kind thoughts
      to a thing,
    it will change
  before your eyes.

JOHN & LYN ST. CLAIR THOMAS
Eyes of the Beholder

Everything
I do and say
with anyone
makes a difference.

GITA BELLIN

Difficulties are opportunities
to better things;
they are stepping stones to greater experience.

Perhaps someday you will be thankful
for some temporary failure
in a particular direction.

When one door closes, another always opens;
as a natural law it has to,
to balance.

BRIAN ADAMS
How To Succeed

If you're into guilt
you're playing God.
The universe is created
so it's O.K. to make a mistake.

If you feel guilty about
what you have done,
you're saying
it's not O.K.
to make mistakes.

To change one's life:

· Start immediately

· Do it flamboyantly

· No exceptions (no excuses)

WILLIAM JAMES

By going along with feelings,
   you unify
      your emotional,
         mental,
            and bodily states.

When you try to fight
   or deny them,
   you divorce yourself
from the reality of your being.

JANE ROBERTS
The Nature of Personal Reality

To be
upset
over what
you don't have...

is
to waste
what
you do have.

KEN KEYES, JR
Handbook to Higher Consciousness

Do the thing

and you will

have the Power.

RALPH WALDO EMERSON

The people
we are in relationship
with are always a mirror,
reflecting our own beliefs,
and simultaneously
we are mirrors,
reflecting their beliefs.

So relationship is one
of the most powerful tools for growth...
if we look honestly at our
relationships we can see so much
about how we
have created them.

SHAKTI GAWAIN
Creative Visualisation

There are
   always risks
      in freedom.

            The only risk
            in bondage
            is that
            of breaking free.

GITA BELLIN

Thoughts
are like
boomerangs.

EILEEN CADDY
The Dawn of Change

The most powerful thing
you can do to change the world,
is to change your own beliefs
about the nature of life, people,
reality, to something
more positive...
and begin to act
accordingly.

SHAKTI GAWAIN
Creative Visualisation

Be not the slave of your own past—
plunge into the sublime seas,
dive deep, and swim far,
so you shall come back
with self-respect,
with new power,
with an advanced experience,
that shall explain
and overlook
the old.

RALPH WALDO EMERSON

There is little sense in attempting
to change external conditions,
you must first change inner beliefs,
then outer conditions
will change accordingly.

BRIAN ADAMS
How To Succeed

The only way to deal
with the future
is to function efficiently
in the Now.

GITA BELLIN

All the world's a stage,
And all the men and women,
merely players;
They have their exits
and their entrances,
And one man in his time
plays many parts.

SHAKESPEARE
As You Like It

Stop sitting there
    with your hands folded
    looking on, doing nothing;

Get into action
    and live this full
            and glorious life.

Now.

You have to do it.

EILEEN CADDY
The Dawn of Change

Doubt is a pain
too lonely to know
that faith
is his twin brother.

KAHLIL GIBRAN
The Prophet

There is no separation
between us and God -
we are divine expressions
of the creative principle ...
there can be no real lack or scarcity;
there is nothing we have to try
to achieve or attract;
we contain the potential
for everything
within us.

SHAKTI GAWAIN
Creative Visualisation

See every difficulty
as a challenge,
a stepping stone,
and never be defeated
by anything
or anyone.

EILEEN CADDY
The Dawn of Change

Success depends
on where intention
is.

GITA BELLIN

If you shut your door
to all errors
truth will be
shut out.

RABINDRANATH TAGORE

Life is like a wild tiger.
You can either lie down
*   and let it*
Lay its paw on your head –
Or sit on its back and ride it.

RIDE THE WILD TIGER

Your subconscious mind has the answer.

If you are confronted with a problem
and you cannot see an immediate answer,
assume that your subconscious has the
solution and is waiting to reveal it to you.

If an answer does not come, turn the
problem over to your deeper mind
prior to sleep. Keep on turning your request
over to your subconscious until the
answer comes.

The response will be a certain 'feeling',
an inner awareness, whereby you
'know' what to do. Guidance in all things
comes as the still small voice within:
It reveals all.

BRIAN ADAMS
How To Succeed

Faith is an oasis
in the heart
which will never be reached
by the caravan of
thinking.

KAHLIL GIBRAN
Sand and Foam

'Everytime we say
"I must do something"
it takes an incredible
amount of energy.

'Far more
than physically
doing it.

GITA BELLIN

Be realistic:
Plan for a miracle.

BHAGWAN SHREE RAJNEESH

We are members
of a vast cosmic orchestra.
in which each living instrument
is essential to the
complementary and
harmonious
playing of
the
whole.

J. ALLEN BOONE
Kinship With All Life

Go confidently
in the direction of your dreams!
Live the life you've imagined.

As you simplify your life,
the laws of the universe
will be simpler;
solitude will not be solitude,
poverty will not be poverty,
nor weakness weakness.

HENRY DAVID THOREAU

What things soever ye desire,
when ye pray,
believe that ye receive them,
and ye shall have them.

MARK 11:24

Giving means extending one's Love with no conditions, no expectations and no boundaries.

Peace of mind occurs, therefore when we put all our attention into giving and have no desire to get anything from, or to change, another person.

The giving motivation leads to a sense of inner peace and joy that is unrelated to time.

GERALD G. JAMPOLSKY
Love is Letting Go of Fear

The only successful manifestation
is one which brings about a change
or growth in consciousness:
that is, it has manifested God,
or revealed him more fully,
as well as having
manifested a form...

DAVID SPANGLER
Manifestation

One may not
          reach the dawn
save by
     the path
          of the night.

KAHLIL GIBRAN
Sand and Foam

We can only be here now
when we accept instantly
our moment-by-moment
emotional experience.

GITA BELLIN

We are not here just to survive
and live long...
We are here to live and know life
in its multi-dimensions
to know life in its richness,
in all its variety.

And when a man lives
multi-dimensionally,
explores all possibilities available,
never shrinks back from any challenge,
goes, rushes to it, welcomes it,
rises to the occasion
then life becomes a flame,
life blooms.

BHAGWAN SHREE RAJNEESH
The Sacred Yes

Your pain
is the breaking
of the shell
that encloses
your understanding.

KAHLIL GIBRAN
The Prophet

*You should always
be aware that your
head creates
your world.*

KEN KEYES, J R.
Handbook to Higher Consciousness

Men are disturbed not by things
that happen,
but by their opinion of the things
that happen.

EPICTETUS

Gratitude
  helps you to grow and expand;
  gratitude brings joy
  and laughter into your lives
  and into the lives of all those
            around you.

EILEEN CADDY
The Dawn of Change

You are never asked
to do more than you are able
without being given
the strength and ability
to do it.

EILEEN CADDY
The Dawn of Change

If one desires a change,
one must be that change
before that change
can take place.

GITA BELLIN

A changed thought system can reverse cause-and-effect as we have known it. For most of us, this is a very difficult concept to accept, because of our resistance to relinquishing the predictability of our past belief system and to assuming responsibility for our thoughts, feelings and reactions.

Since we always look within before looking out, we can perceive attack outside us only when we have first accepted attack as real within.

GERALD G. JAMPOLSKY
Love is Letting Go of Fear

Be outrageous !

People who
achieve mastery
have the ability
to be outrageous.

GITA BELLIN

The divinest things - religion, love, truth, beauty, justice - seem to lose their meaning and value when we sink into lassitude and indifference...

It is a signal that we should quit meditation and books and go out into the open air, into the presence of nature, into the company of flocks and children, where we may drink new health and vigour from the clear and full-flowing fountains of life, afar from the arid wastes of theory and speculation; where we may learn again that it is not by intellectual questionings, but by believing, hoping, loving, and doing that man finds joy and peace.

JOHN LANCASTER SPALDING

Expect the best;
    convert problems into opportunities;
Be dissatisfied with the status quo;
    Focus on where you want to go,
        instead of where you're coming from;
and most importantly,
    Decide to be happy,
        Knowing it's an attitude,
            a habit gained from daily practice,
                and not a result or payoff.

DENIS WAITLEY
The Winner's Edge

Everyone
and everything
around you
is your
teacher.

KEN KEYES, JR
Handbook to Higher Consciousness

Peace of mind
  comes from not wanting
    to change others,
      but by simply accepting them
        as they are.

True acceptance
  is always without demands
    and expectations.

GERALD G. JAMPOLSKY
Love is Letting Go of Fear

To hate another is to hate yourself.
We all live within the one Universal Mind.
What we think about another,
we think about ourselves.

If you have an enemy, forgive him now.
Let all bitterness and resentment dissolve.
You owe your fellow man love;
show him love, not hate.

Show charity and goodwill toward others
and it will return to enhance
your own life
in many wonderful ways.

BRIAN ADAMS
How To Succeed

*Disillusionment
with yourself
must precede
Enlightenment.*

VERNON HOWARD
The Mystic Path to Cosmic Power

Love
   is a space
    in which
    all other emotions
  can be experienced.

ROBERT PRINABLE

Before enlightenment
  chopping wood
  carrying water.

After enlightenment
  chopping wood
  carrying water.

ZEN PROVERB

The measure of mental health
is the disposition to find good
everywhere.

RALPH WALDO EMERSON

Truth does not change
although
   your perception of it
   may vary
   or alter
      drastically.

JOHN & LYN ST. CLAIR THOMAS
Eyes of the Beholder

Learn your lessons
                quickly,

and move on.

EILEEN CADDY
The Dawn of Change

Life has its sleep, its periods of
inactivity, when it loses its movements,
takes no new food, living upon its past
storage. Then it grows helpless, its
muscles relaxed, and it easily lends
itself to be jeered at for its stupour.

In the rhythm of life, pauses there
must be for the renewal of life. Life
in its activity is ever spending itself,
burning all its fuel.

This extravagance cannot go on
indefinitely, but is always followed
by a passive stage, when all expendi-
ture is stopped and all adventures
abandoned in favour of rest and
slow recuperation.

RABINDRANATH TAGORE

People with high self esteem have it
    because they have overcome their failures.

They have been put to the test of life,
    overcome the problems
        and grown.

DAVID JANSEN

The fastest way
to freedom
is to
feel
your feelings.

GITA BELLIN

Do not take life's experiences
too seriously. Above all, do not
let them hurt you, for in reality
they are nothing but
dream experiences....

If circumstances are bad
and you have to bear them,
do not make them
a part of yourself.

Play your part in life,
but never forget that
it is only a role.

PARAMAHANSA YOGANANDA
Par-a-gram

The snow goose
  need not bathe
    to make itself white.

      Neither need you
        do anything
          but be yourself.

LAO-TSE

Be like a very small
              joyous child
living gloriously in the
              ever present Now
without a single worry or concern
about even the next
              moment of time.

EILEEN CADDY
The Dawn of Change

There is but one cause
of human failure
and that is
man's lack of faith
in his true Self.

WILLIAM JAMES

We are injured and hurt emotionally
~ not so much by other people
or what they say or don't say ~
but by our own attitude
and our own response.

MAXWELL MALTZ
Psycho-Cybernetics

Until
you can understand
that nothing can happen to you,
nothing can ever come to you
or be kept from you,
except in accord
with your state
of consciousness,
you do not have
the key to life.

PAUL TWITCHELL
The Flute of God
ECKANKAR

If you depend on someone
for your happiness
you are becoming a slave,
you are becoming dependent,
you are creating a bondage.

And you depend on
so many people; they all
become subtle masters,
they all exploit you in return.

BHAGWAN SHREE RAJNEESH
The Book of the Books Vol. IV

Be not heedful of the morrow,
but rather gaze upon today,
for sufficient for today
is the miracle thereof.

Be not overmindful
of yourself when you give
but be mindful of the necessity.
For every giver himself receives from
the Father, and that much more
abundantly.

ANNIE BESANT
Some Difficulties of the Inner Life

Life's fulfillment finds constant contradictions in its path; but those are necessary for the sake of its advance.

The stream is saved from the sluggishness of its current by the perpetual opposition of the soil through which it must cut its way. It is the soil which forms its banks.

The Spirit of fight belongs to the genius of life.

RABINDRANATH TAGORE

Take heart,
   truth and happiness
      will get you in the end.

You can't lose in this game.

Have fun.

It goes on too long
   to be taken seriously
      all the time.

JOHN & LYN ST. CLAIR THOMAS
Eyes of the Beholder

How wonderful is the way in which, with quite ordinary folk, power leaps to our aid in any time of emergency. We lead timid lives, shrinking from difficult tasks till perhaps we are forced into them or ourselves determine on them, and immediately we seem to unlock the unseen forces. When we have to face danger, then courage comes, when trial puts a long-continued strain upon us, we find ourselves possessed by the power to endure; if when disaster ultimately brings the fall which we so long dreaded, we feel underneath us the strength as of the everlasting arms. Common experience teaches that, when great demands are made upon us, if only we fearlessly accept the challenge and confidently expend our strength, every danger or difficulty brings its own strength - "As thy days so shall thy strength be."

J. A. HADFIELD
The Psychology of Power

Work
    is love
        made visible.

KAHLIL GIBRAN
The Prophet

All things are in the act of change;
thou thyself in ceaseless transformation
and partial decay,
and the whole universe
with thee.

MARCUS AURELIUS ANTONIUS

Man has falsely identified
    himself with the pseudo-soul
        or ego.
When he transfers his sense
    of identity to his true being,
    the immortal Soul,
    he discovers that
    all pain is unreal.
            He no longer
                can even imagine
                the state of suffering.

PARAMAHANSA YOGANANDA
Sayings of Paramahansa Yogananda

How soon
  will you realise
  that the only thing
  you don't have is
  the direct experience

    that there's
    nothing you need

that you
don't have ?

KEN KEYES, JR
Handbook to Higher Consciousness

Regrets
can hold you back
and can prevent the most
wonderful things
taking place
in your
lives.

EILEEN CADDY
Footprints on the Path

You will have
    wonderful surges forward.
Then there must be
  a time of consolidating
  before the next forward surge.

  Accept this
    as part of the process
    and never become
        downhearted.

EILEEN CADDY
God Spoke to Me

Don't try to force anything.
Let life be a deep let-go.

See God opening millions
of flowers every day
without forcing
the buds.

BHAGWAN SHREE RAJNEESH
Dying for Enlightenment

Come to the edge, he said.
They said: We are afraid.
Come to the edge, he said.
They came.
He pushed them...and they flew.

GUILLAUME APOLLINAIRE

Do not be desirous of having
things done quickly. Do not
look at small advantages.
Desire to have things done
quickly prevents their being
done thoroughly. Looking
at small advantages prevents
great affairs from being
accomplished.

CONFUCIUS

... as the springs return -
regardless of time or man -
so is HOPE !
Sometimes but a tiny bud
that has to push up
through the hard shell
of circumstance
to reach the light
of accomplishment.
Do not give up HOPE !

DOROTHY MILLER COLE

You must begin
to trust yourself.

If you do not
then you will forever
be looking to others
to prove your own merit to you,
and you will never be satisfied.

You will always be asking
others what to do,
and at the same time
resenting those
from whom
you seek such aid.

JANE ROBERTS
The Nature of Personal Reality

You know quite well,
deep within you,
that there is only
a single magic,
a single power,
a single salvation ...
and that is called loving.
Well then,
love your suffering.
Do not resist it, do not flee from it
It is only your aversion that hurts,
nothing else.

HERMAN HESSE

'When one realises
one is asleep,
at that moment
one is already half-awake.

P.D. OUSPENSKY &
G.I. GURDJIEFF

We are built to conquer environment,
solve problems, achieve goals,
and we find no real satisfaction
or happiness in life
without obstacles to conquer
and goals to achieve.

MAXWELL MALTZ
Psycho-Cybernetics

Most people don't know
how brave they really are.

In fact, many potential heroes,
both men and women,
live out their lives in self-doubt.

If they only knew they had
these deep resources,
it would help give them the self-reliance
to meet most problems,
even a big crisis.

R.E. CHAMBERS

Realise that you cannot
help a soul unless that soul
really wants help and is
ready to be helped.

I tell you to send that soul
nothing but Love and more Love.

Be still and wait,
but be there when that soul
turns for help.

EILEEN CADDY
God Spoke to Me

No soul that aspires
can ever fail to rise ;
no heart that loves
can ever be abandoned.

Difficulties exist only
that in overcoming them
we may grow strong,
and they only who
who have suffered
are able to save.

ANNIE BESANT
Some Difficulties of the Inner Life

Be aware of the reality of your feelings. As you become more aware of your beliefs over a period of time, you will see how they bring forth certain feelings automatically.

A man who is sure of himself is <u>not</u> angry at every slight done him, nor does he carry grudges. A man who fears for his own worth, however, <u>is</u> furious under such conditions.

The free flow of your emotions will always lead you back to your conscious beliefs if you do not impede them.

JANE ROBERTS
The Nature of Personal Reality

Begin with the possible;
begin with one step.
There is always a limit,
you cannot do more than you can.
If you try to do too much,
you will do nothing.

P. D. OUSPENSKY &
G. I. GURDJIEFF

You must love yourself
before you love another.

By accepting yourself
and joyfully
being what you are,
you fulfill your own abilities,
and your simple presence
can make
others happy.

JANE ROBERTS
The Nature of Personal Reality

Ideas by themselves
cannot produce change of being;
your effort must go in the
right direction,
and one must correspond
to the other.

P. D. OUSPENSKY
G. I. GURDJIEFF

There is much to use of nature's way.
It is with you always,
available to you always.

Take time to hear and see
that which is close at hand.

There are forces in you untried.

They are yours to be used
as you find them.

JOHN & LYN ST·CLAIR-THOMAS
Eyes of the Beholder

You will decide
  on a matter,
  and it will be
  established for you,
  and light will shine
  on your ways.

JOB 22:28

A loving
  person lives
    in
  a loving world

A hostile
  person lives
    in
  a hostile world.

Everyone you meet
  is your mirror.

KEN KEYES, JR
Handbook to Higher Consciousness

All the powers of your inner Self
are set into activation as a result of
your conscious beliefs. You have lost
a sense of responsibility for your
conscious thought because you have
been taught that it is not what forms
your life. You have been told that
regardless of your belief you are
terrorized by unconscious conditioning.
Some of your beliefs originated in
your childhood, but you are not at
their mercy unless you <u>believe</u> that
you are.

JANE ROBERTS
The Nature of Personal Reality

Each player must accept the cards
life deals him or her.

But once they are in hand,
he or she alone must decide
how to play the cards
in order to win the game.

VOLTAIRE

A person who is not disturbed
  by the incessant flow of desires –
  that enter like rivers into the
  ocean, which is ever being
  filled but is always still –
  can alone achieve peace,
  and not the man who strives
  to satisfy such desires.

BHAGAVAD-GITA II:70

Stop looking
  for a scapegoat
    in your life
but be willing
  to face the truth
    within yourself
      and right
        your own wrongs.

EILEEN CADDY
Footprints on the Path

It is important
  from time to time
   to slow down,
    to go away by yourself,
     and simply
       Be.

EILEEN CADDY
The Dawn of Change

Life has a bright side and a dark side,
  for the world of relativity
  is composed of light and shadows.

  If you permit your thoughts
    to dwell on evil,
    you yourself will become ugly.

      Look only for the good
      in everything,
      that you absorb
      the quality of beauty.

PARAMAHANSA YOGANANDA
Sayings of Paramahansa Yogananda

What is of all things most yielding
Can overcome that which is most hard
  Being substanceless, it can enter in
    even where there is no crevice.
  That is how I know the value of
    action which is actionless.
But that there can be teaching
  without words
Value in action which is actionless
  Few indeed can understand.
  That the yielding conquers the resistant
    and the soft conquers the hard
    is a fact known by all
    but utilized by none.

LAO TZU

I know I'm not seeing things
as they are,

I'm seeing things as I am.

Be very very still
and allow every new experience
to take place in your life
without any resistance
whatsoever.

You do not have to do anything,
you simply have to be
and let things happen.

EILEEN CADDY
Footprints on the Path

Not judging is another way
of letting go of fear and experiencing
Love.

When we learn not to judge
others - and totally accept them,
and not want to change them -
we can simultaneously learn to
accept ourselves.

GERALD G. JAMPOLSKY
Love is Letting Go of Fear

The difference between
a flower and a weed
is a judgement.

A man must elevate himself
by his own mind,
not degrade himself.

The mind is the friend
of the conditioned soul,
and his enemy as well.

BHAGAVAD-GITA VI:5

Every end
is a new
beginning.

Acknowledgements

Especially I wish to thank Malcolm Cohan for his love, and constant encouragement without which this book would have never been started, sustained or completed.

I would like to thank Margo Snape for her beautiful artwork for the cover; and to Shane McCoy for his wonderful illustrations.

Further, I would like to express my deepest thanks to my family and friends whose presence in my life contributed, whether directly or indirectly, towards the book.

Finally, I would like to acknowledge all the great spirits I have quoted in this book whose words have given so much to my understanding and growth.

I am grateful to the publishers who kindly gave me permission to reproduce copyright material. These quotations were extracted from the following publications:

BRIAN ADAMS, *How To Succeed*, Copyright © 1985 by Brian Adams. Published by Melvin Powers Wilshire Book Company, California, USA.

GITA BELLIN & THE SELF-TRANSFORMATION CENTRE, *A Sharing of Completion*, Copyright © 1983 Self-Transformation Seminars Ltd.

J. ALLEN BOONE, *Kinship With All Life*, Copyright © 1954 by Harper & Row, Publishers, Inc., New York. By permission of the Publisher.

ASHLEIGH BRILLIANT, *I Have Abandoned My Search For Truth And Am Now Looking For A Good Fantasy*, Copyright © 1980 Ashleigh Brilliant, Woodbridge Press, California.

EILEEN CADDY, *The Dawn of Change*, Copyright © 1979 The Findhorn Press, *God Spoke To Me*, Copyright © 1971 The Findhorn Press, *Footprints On The Path*, Copyright © 1976 Eileen Caddy.